when Hello means Goodbye

D0106774

A Guide For Parents
Whose Child Dies Before Birth,
At Birth Or Shortly After Birth

by

Pat Schwiebert, RN
Director,
Perinatal Loss

Paul Kirk, MD
Professor and Chairman
Department of Obstetrics and Gynecology
Oregon Health Sciences University

1

With gratitude and humility we dedicate this booklet to the families who have been our teachers, especially Peg Swanton, Jude Kerr, Kathy McNassar and David and Kathryn Castricano.

ABOUT THIS BOOK

It's been thirteen years since we wrote the first edition of When Hello Means Goodbye. Since then there has been considerable change in the general understanding and appreciation of the needs of bereaved parents. We've seen real improvement in the ability of medical, religious, and other professionals to help bereaved parents deal with their loss. And, thanks to the informal education which doctors, nurses and others have received from listening to bereaved parents, hospital policies around the country are now less likely to treat infant loss only as a medical misfortune and more likely to view it as the human tragedy that it is.

What has not changed during these years is our certainty of your need as a bereaved parent to be acknowledged for your loss, and to see your infant recognized and appreciated as a real person–a person whose death is to be mourned no less than that of any older child.

In the first edition of When Hello Means Goodbye we attempted to provide a primer for people who were unfamiliar with grief, to offer words of comfort to the bereaved and to assure parents like you who are now reading this booklet that the emotional reactions that follow the death of a child are indeed normal and necessary. These objective are retained in the second and third editions.

In our second edition we added photographs. We were a bit anxious about how the pictures would be accepted, but what we suspected proved to be true: parents who had no photographs of their own used our pictures to help them remember their own dead child. And other parents reported that seeing these pictures was what gave them the permission they needed to take their own photographs, while it was still possible to do so, without feeling that their desire to do so was somehow unusual or strange.

We hope that the minor improvements in this third edition will make it an even more valuable resource to you.

We offer this booklet as a companion, to be with you in the journey of grief which is uniquely yours. By no means does it contain all the answers. And, unfortunately it cannot protect you from the emotional hurt which you may experience along the way, because of the comments and behavior of well-meaning but insensitive and uninformed persons who have no idea what you are going through. But if this book makes your journey even a little easier, because it helps anticipate some of the perils ahead, we will know it has served its purpose.

WHEN HELLO MEANS GOODBYE

STILLBORN

I carried you in hope,
the long nine months of my term,
remembered that close hour when we made you,
often felt you kick and move
as slowly you grew within me,
wondered what you would look like
when your wet head emerged,
girl or boy, and at what glad moment
I should hear your birth cry,
and I welcoming you
with all you needed of warmth and food;
we had a home waiting for you.

After my strong labourings,
sweat cold on my limbs,
my small cries merging with the summer air,
you came. You did not cry.
You did not breathe.
We had not expected this;
it seems your birth had no meaning,
or had you rejected us?

They will say that you did not live,
register you as stillborn.
But you lived for me all that time
in the dark chamber of my womb,
and when I think of you now,
perfect in your little death,
I know that for me you are born still;
I shall carry you with me forever,
my child, you were always mine,
you are mine now.

Death and life are the same mysteries.

Leonard Clark

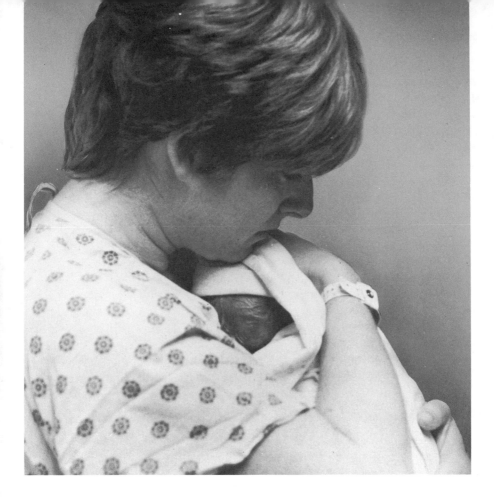

Dear Parents,

My son Tony died three weeks ago, died before he was born. When there was absolutely no hope left that he was alive I told the doctor that I wanted to see and hold my baby right now. I wanted desperately to still be a mother, to hold my baby and know for myself the truth of his death. But I was afraid. There was no magic way to be delivered of my baby or of the pain of knowing. To be a mother meant to give birth to my son even though he was dead.

After the final word came that indeed my baby's life had ended, David and I left the hospital for a while to be alone. When we returned I remember walking across the hospital parking lot seeing the trees, feeling the cool crisp autumn wind, and thinking how I'd rather take a nice long walk to just about anywhere else. I wanted to walk away from all the pain.

6

At the same time I wanted to see and know my baby's face and body before the effect of death would change him. *Who was he?* I needed to know. So we went back in to the hospital - to prepare for induced labor.

It took two days for birth to happen. You might think this would be a nightmare time, a horrible waiting. It wasn't. It was a time of planning and sharing. The people who shared my life and pregnancy came offering their hugs and tears. The gift of their tears was precious. David felt that as each person departed a little piece of pain departed too leaving love and caring in its place.

Because I had read **When Hello Means Goodbye** in the past and had worked with mothers and their babies, I knew that I wanted to make special the only time we would have with Tony. For me this meant holding, bathing, and dressing Tony and sharing Tony's birth with my family.

The greatest gift I can give to you, the reader of this book, is to say, "Be your child's parent." Take this little bit of time you have with your baby and be this child's mom and dad. Let your parental feelings guide you in the same ways you would if the child were alive.

The pain of birth/death is deep, almost unbearable. But there is peace in formally acknowledging this particular baby as your child and you as its parent. This knowing will get you through the difficult days ahead. Others may want to spare you pain, and take away the pain you already feel. They simply cannot do it. Please trust in yourselves to be able to handle grief. Trust the people who wrote this book. Trust the parents who have gone through a similar experience before. There is meaning in your child's life and death.

We had several days of knowing that our son was dead, before he was delivered. We had time to plan how we would arrange to celebrate his brief time with us. And we had people around us who anticipated our needs and desires.

How glad we are now that one of our friends had the foresight to snap pictures during the three hours we spent holding and loving Tony. These pictures are a blessing which we gladly share with you here.

Love,

Tony's mom

Kathryn Castricano

7

HOLD CLOSE THESE MOMENTS
FOR WE SHALL ALWAYS LIVE
BY REMEMBERING

The idea for this book was conceived while working with parents whose babies had died, and hearing them say over and over again, "if only we had known." They wished that they had made better use of the limited time they had with their offspring, taking advantage of every opportunity to gather reminders that they would be able to treasure later. They wished they had known what kinds of reactions to expect from their friends and neighbors. They wished they had been able to anticipate the kinds of feelings they would experience during the normal process of grief.

We want to help you to "know." Nothing in this book will take away the pain and hurt you are now feeling. Nothing anyone can say will do that, though well meaning people will want to try. But at least this book will let you know what we have learned from other bereaved parents about how they felt physically, and emotionally, where they found their greatest support, what means they discovered to help them celebrate their baby's birth and death, and what experiences helped them make it through their ordeal.

Within a very short time you will have to begin dealing with many feelings that are probably new to you. There will also be many decisions that you will need to face. Since your hospital stay will probably be too short to allow time for the staff to prepare you for everything that is ahead of you, this book is designed to at least suggest some questions to ask and to provide you with a list of resource people in the community who are ready to offer help. We hope this book will keep you from later having to say, "if only we had known."

As you read this book you will notice that we refer to the death of your child very openly and in a positive way. This is intentional on our part. Our experience with parents convinces us that you will manage your grief much better if you can face the death squarely, rather than avoiding or postponing it, or pretending that your child never really lived.

The truth is that parents don't forget, nor do they want to forget their offspring, even if the only life the child experienced was in the mother's womb. If you ask an 84-year-old woman, "how many children do you have," she will probably answer something like this: "I have eight children. Two of them

8

died at birth, one died of pneumonia when he was four, and the others are as healthy as oxen."

Although it is normal to want to run away from much of what is happening to you right now, later you will be glad you chose instead to deal directly with your situation, even to the point of treasuring and gathering memories of your child's birth and death days.

Like other people you are bound to feel grief at the loss of someone who is very special to you. And the more significant the loss, the "better" the grief. Grief is the process that you must go through in order to readjust your life to the loss.

THE MAIN THING IN LIFE
IS NOT TO BE
AFRAID
TO BE HUMAN
Pablo Casals

FEELINGS

At this time of loss you will find yourself experiencing a number of confusing, bewildering feelings. These feelings are the basis of grief, a normal process you must go through in order to come to terms with the loss of your baby. You will have both physical and emotional symptoms. Though these symptoms will be distressing and painful, they will not indicate that you are "going out of your mind." But at times you may feel as though you are crossing some very stormy waters all alone.

Always remember that there is a purpose behind the grief process—to allow you formally and appropriately to detach yourself from the relationship you have formed with your baby over the past few months. This is not to say that the process will encourage you to "forget the past." Rather it will help you to reach the stage where you can remember this experience, understand it, accept it, and then look forward to the future.

There is no standard response, no acceptable or unacceptable form of behavior that you will be expected to follow. Nor is there a particular time frame in which you will be encouraged to have accomplished the task of "letting go."

9

Everyone must do the grief work in his or her own time. But for most people the process will take longer than they ever would have expected. We just don't get over something as important as a person's life that easily or quickly.

Do not feel that you have to have all the sensations and experiences that are described in this book. Do not worry that something is wrong with you just because you don't behave in a certain way or experience a particular emotion. Though your emotions at this time may be more intense than any you have ever experienced before, don't be afraid of them.

Though no one can ever measure one person's pain against that of another, most people assume that the loss of a child is the deepest loss that any person can experience. There are good reasons for this assumption. You expect to lose your parents, but you do not expect to lose your child. Your child is an extension of yourself. Your future plans have included the child. Your role as a parent—to provide for, to protect, and to nurture—has been left unfulfilled.

One problem you will face in connection with the loss of your child is your lonliness in grief. No one else knew this person but you, the parents. To other people it may seem like you are grieving over the loss of a non-person. They will soon forget, while you will continue to remember, your child's impact on your life.

WHEN YOUR PARENT DIES YOU'VE LOST YOUR PAST BUT WHEN YOUR CHILD DIES YOU'VE LOST YOUR FUTURE

PHYSICAL SYMPTOMS

What are some of the physical symptoms that are a part of the grief process? There may be a feeling of severe physical exhaustion, perhaps further aggravated by a difficult delivery. You may feel a heaviness in your chest, a need to take deep sighing breaths, palpitations, "butterflies in the stomach" and aching arms. You may lose your appetite and you may have dreams and nightmares. Most, if not all of these symptoms are a part of the initial grief process and they will disappear with time.

In the past, medication has been used much too freely in times of initial grief. Running away from the pain you are feeling, or being tranquilized so that you don't sob too much only postpones and prolongs your real pain. It is better to face what must be faced now while your family and friends are close by.

It is important that you get a good night's rest. A light night sedation, if you are having difficulty sleeping, is probably all the medication you will need, and then only for a few days.

In grief, one can endure the day, just the day. But when one also tries to bear the grief ahead, one cannot compass it. As for happiness, it can only be the ability to experience the moment. It is not next year that life will be so flawless and if we keep trying to wait for next year's happiness, the river of time will wind past and we shall not have lived at all.

EMOTIONS

You will probably pass through a whole series of emotions. They will not always occur in the order that we list here; they will not always be felt with the same intensity; and sometimes they will be missing altogether. Also you may think that you are finished experiencing a certain kind of emotion that you associate with a particular stage in the grief process only to one day find yourself back to it again. Some days you will feel quite well and other days you will find yourself down again.

You will feel a great sense of loss, emptiness. The fact that you are obviously no longer pregnant may highlight the emptiness. Your body will try to function as if the baby were still alive—e.g. your breasts may become engorged as they make milk—and this can seem cruel and bewildering.

You will also feel a sense of alarm and restlessness. C.S. Lewis once wrote,"No one ever told me that grief felt so like fear." It will be difficult to settle back to your usual routine. Activities that used to interest you, you may no longer find appealing. Your ability to concentrate on simple tasks may be diminished for a time. Simple decisions may be difficult to make. Just deciding what to prepare for dinner, or what to wear may seem overwhelming to you.

Forgetfulness may be another disturbing part of grief for you. This will be especially noticeable if you plunge yourself back into work or take on major responsibilities too soon.

11

Life will seem out of control and you will feel extremely vulnerable. *Babies aren't supposed to die. This wasn't supposed to happen to me. How can I ever be certain about anything ever again? What's the point in planning for the future?*

You may feel invisible to others, especially in large crowds. Because others cannot see the pain that is encompassing you, you will imagine that they cannot see you. You may find yourself staring out the window and wondering how the rest of the world can continue as if nothing has happened, when you feel as though your whole world has stopped.

You may feel very angry. It will probably seem very unfair that your baby has died. "Why did this happen to me?" you will ask. You have every right to feel angry. You have lost something very special.

Whether or not there is a satisfactory medical reason for the death, you will still feel angry and hurt, and perhaps hostile. You may take out this anger on the people very close to you—your spouse, your family, your friends. You may blame God, the nurses, the physicians, or others who have been involved in the care of your pregnancy.

WHEN PEOPLE ASK YOU "AM I RIGHT TO BE ANGRY?", HAVE YOU THOUGHT OF ASKING THEM, "AM I RIGHT TO BE THIRSTY?"

Theodore Isaac Rubin

Guilt is an emotion that is usually felt more deeply by grieving parents than by others who are grieving over the death of a close friend or family member. This guilt stems from the tendency for parents to see themselves as "super-parents" — persons who are fully capable of fulfilling all the duties of provider, protector and nurturer of their children.

If your child dies you will find your image of yourself as a super-parent shattered. You will experience more guilt than is justified by the actual situation. Even with as much assurance that others can give you that you did not cause the death, and could not have prevented it, you may find yourself wondering: *Could it have been that I didn't observe the correct diet?* or *"If I hadn't worked so hard during the last few weeks of the pregnancy would my baby have survived?"* or *"Was the death*

12

caused when we made love and I started to bleed?"

Guilt is the self doubt in us rising to the surface. It is a sense of anguish that comes from not achieving what we set out to achieve.

THE QUALITY OF A PERSON'S LIFE CANNOT BE JUDGED BY OUR LIMITED UNDERSTANDING OF TIME.

You may also find that you feel guilty *because* you are suffering deep grief over the death of your child. Statements made by well-meaning friends may cause you to question the validity of your deep feelings of sorrow—statements like the following: "Just be glad you didn't get to know her. This way you won't have to suffer the grief." or "The woman down the street lost all of her children in a fire. You are lucky compared with her."

The fact is that you cannot measure your grief against the grief of another. Your grief will not lessen, just because the grief of another person is perceived to be greater.

Another comment you may hear is this: "You are young. You can always have another baby." The speaker assumes that this child can be replaced by another child, like an ailing house plant can be replaced by a healthy one. You may indeed give birth to another child. But this will be *another* child, not a substitute for the one who has died.

A PERSON'S A PERSON
NO MATTER HOW SMALL
Dr. Seuss

PLEASE DON'T TELL THEM YOU NEVER
GOT TO KNOW ME

It is I whose kicks you will always remember,
  I who gave you heartburn that a dragon would envy,
  I who couldn't seem to tell time and got your days and
nights mixed up,
It is I who acknowledged your craving for peach ice cream by
  knocking the cold bowl off your belly,
  I who went shopping and helped you pick out the "perfect"
  teddy bear for me,
  I who liked to be cradled in your belly and rocked off to
  dreamy slumber by the fire,
It is I who never had a doubt about your love,
It is I who was able to put a lifetime of joy into an instant.

Pat Schwiebert

14

THERE IS NOTHING WRONG WITH CRYING

Actually, crying is an excellent way to release built-up tension, and you will no doubt experience plenty of this. A problem for you may be that your friends will not know what to do when you cry. They may feel self conscious about being with you while you are crying, and may even avoid mentioning the baby for fear this may cause you to cry. You may feel self conscious too, especially when the tears come suddenly and without warning.

But crying is okay. You can help your friends understand your need to cry and thank them for allowing you this opportunity. They will be relieved to know that you are glad they are with you even if you do cry a lot.

As time goes by you will find that you cry less and less when you talk to people, or when you think about your baby. Don't worry about whether you are crying too much or too little. Crying is not a measure of how much you loved your baby, but rather an indication of how completely you allow yourself to openly express yourself.

CRYING HELPS GET THE SAD AND THE MAD OUT OF YOU. CRYING IS LIKE GENTLE MELTING

YOUR BODY DOES NOT KNOW
YOUR BABY DIED

It seems very cruel that nature will take you through the same physical discomforts common to all women who have just given birth.

You will have a discharge called "lochia" for approximately two weeks. At first it will require a pad change every few hours.

Each day the discharge should lessen and begin to appear brownish. If you attempt too much activity before your body has been given adequate time to heal you will notice that your flow will become too much. Slow down. Put your feet up. If, after a few hours, the flow hasn't stopped, call your doctor. You can expect that your menstrual cycle will resume within the first two months.

15

Your breasts may fill with milk. Your body is preparing itself for nursing. The best way to stop the manufacture of milk is to prevent stimulation of the nipples. When you take a shower don't let the water strike the nipples. Wear a tight fitting bra. Limit fluid intake. If you have nursed a baby before you may experience aching in your breasts, especially when you are around other babies. If you are uncomfortable due to engorgement, ice packs applied to your breasts and Tylenol II tabs every four hours as needed will help.

If you had an episiotomy you may be uncomfortable for a few days while the stitches heal. A warm bath will be soothing.

Another sensation common to most moms is feeling the baby kick long after the baby has been born. Mothers grow accustomed to this feeling throughout their pregnancy. Don't be afraid of these lingering sensations. Remember the "kicking times" with joy for the life that was there.

Lacy

Everyone's forgotten you, Lacy.
Everyone but me . . .

Your mother, a mother without
a child. What am I? I had
a baby, but she's gone. Am
I a mother? What am I?

Sue Chaidez

I Wonder

Did she look like you, or
did she look like me?
Coal black hair, blue eyes.
Formed perfectly. So they say.
Why didn't I see for myself?

I thought it'd be too hard
But now it's even harder
Stangers saw. I needed to see.
Why not me? I was her mother.

I should have known.
But now I can only wonder. . . .

Mary Rose

16

TAKING A PICTURE OF YOUR BABY

Though the intense pain which you feel will lessen with the passing of time you won't ever want to forget this little person who was so dear to you, and you may be afraid you won't remember what your baby looked like. A picture can provide tangible evidence that this was your child – that he or she was indeed a part of your life, and equal to your other children in love you gave, if while only inside you. And it can relieve your fears that time will dim your memory.

We can arrange for a picture of your baby to be taken in the nursery in the same way as with living babies after they are cleaned and dressed. Even if you decide now that you don't want to see or keep the picture, it can be placed with the baby's hospital record, and you may request a copy at a later time if you change your mind, or you may want to take your own pictures. The use of a Polaroid camera, or of the one-hour photo processing available in most towns, will help relieve any worries you may have about how the pictures will turn out.

Keep in mind when taking the pictures, you are taking pictures of your child, not a specimen.

THERE IS ONLY ONE BEAUTIFUL CHILD IN THE WORLD AND EVERY PARENT HAS IT

SEEING AND HOLDING YOUR BABY

Often parents are afraid of viewing their dead child because of what the imagine the child will look like. A parent may say, "We would rather picture our baby in our minds as if she were alive." We have found however, that when parents only imagine what the dead child looks like, they later develop distorted notions which may cause even worse feelings that crowd our the vision that they are trying to maintain. The fact is that parents are usually relieved and pleased when they do take the opportunity to see their baby. They almost always find out that the baby's actual appearance – as if in sleep – is far more comforting that any fantasy that they would have had to depend on their minds to create. It has been humbling for us to discover that parents see their babies through "different eyes" than do their more objective caregivers.

GOD'S OWN CREATION
FRAMED WITH PEACEFULNESS

If you are not sure you want to see the baby, ask the nurse to describe the baby to you. This may help you to decide.

Would you like to hold your baby? Many parents have treasured the opportunity to take their child in their arms while they said their goodbyes, and there is nothing wrong with wanting to do this. Think it over. You may later wish that you had asked for this opportunity while it was still available.

The nurse can wrap your baby in a blanket and bring him or her to your room if you wish, and you can decide then if, and for how long, your will hold the baby. Let the nurse know if you want the nurse to stay with you or if you prefer to be left alone with your baby.

KEEPSAKES

You may want to collect some or all of the following as further reminders of your child. Not all hospitals will automatically provide these unless you ask, so make a point of telling the staff which of these are important to you.

- a lock of hair (not all babies are born with hair no matter how old they are)
- a set of footprints and handprints
- a birth certificate
- a picture of your baby
- the plastic arm bracelet prepared by the hospital to identify your child
- a small scrap of paper from the fetal monitoring showing a tracing of your baby's heart rate
- a record of the weight, length, and head and chest measurements of your baby
- the receiving blanket your baby was first wrapped in

Some parents have found that several well spent hours with their stillborn child can provide precious memories for the days and weeks to come. here is a list of some of the things parents have chosen to do during these hours:
- hold their baby
- bathe their baby
- dress their baby in a special outfit
- talk to their baby or sing her a lullaby

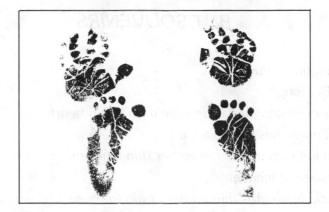

- invite family and friends in to see their baby
- rock their baby
- have someone take pictures of them with their baby
- just sit together and hold the baby and cry

Some of these suggestions may seem strange to you. They are only listed to show you how some parents have chosen to spend their brief time with their baby. You must choose for yourself what you think will be helpful to you down the road.

Performing these physical activities may help to satisfy some of your intense desires to care for your baby, the same desires which you anticipated when you still expected the baby to be born alive. The fact that the child is dead does not automatically diminish your need to cradle, and speak words of love to him or her.

HUMAN BEINGS SHOULD NOT DIE WITHOUT THEIR NAMES BEING REMEMBERED OR ELSE HUMAN BEINGS DON'T COUNT

YOUR CHILD DESERVES A NAME

We strongly encourage you to give your baby a name, preferably the name you had been planning for the child all along. Don't "save" the name for your next child. It rightly belongs to this one.

Names are important. You will use the name as you talk about this little person to others. You will use it as you tell your other children about this special child in your life. You will find it easier to connect your memories to this child if you can refer to him or her by name.

19

BUT SOUVENIRS

Daughters may die,
   But why?
For even daughters can't live with half a heart.
   Three days isn't much a life.
But long enough to remember thin blue lips, uneven
   gasps in incubators,
Racking breaths that cause a pain to those who watched.
   Long enough to remember I never held her
Or felt her softness
   Or counted her toes.
I didn't even know the color of her eyes.
   Dead paled hands not quite covered by the gown she
Was to go home in.
   Moist earthy smell.
One small casket.
   And the tears.
You see, I hold in my hand but souvenirs of an occasion.
   A sheet of paper filled with statistics,
A certificate with smudged footprints,
   A tiny bracelet engraved "Girl, Smith."
You say that you are sorry
   That you know how I feel.
But you can't know because I don't feel.
   Not yet.

Anonymous

MICAELEE

We planned and waited so long for you
Then, after all the times of tests and temperatures
At last you began to live in me.
I listened to your speedy little heart and
Imagined who you would be.
As I snuggled up against your Daddy
You kicked him "hello" that first time.

Every decision was made with such great care,
What color to paint, a quilt to sew,
A rocker for late night feedings,
Even a gown for your christening.
You waited patiently an extra week
So every detail could be completed.
Six years of anticipation for you.

We headed for the hospital, hurting,
But happy that your time had come.
We'd finally meet our little girl.
We did everything right, breathing,
Relaxing, pushing, panting.
How were we to know that when last I snuggled
Your kick to Dad had meant "good-bye."

Peggy Swanton

Hello, little son.

I was so afraid to finally meet you. When you died two days ago inside of me, I was afraid you would not be someone I could recognize and know. Forgive my fears.

The first thing I notice are the birth bruises that any prematurely born infant might have. And there is so much blonde hair on your little head. David put a little stocking cap on your head to hide the molding of your skull bones. I know it is a change that comes with death, but also that it's because you are small and were born before your time. Your eyes are closed and puffy. If only you would look up at me. Your mouth is open, with a crimson color to your lips. David thinks you look a lot like your brother. It takes two hands to hold your limp head and body. It is a perfect little body, warm and soft with all the right number of fingers and toes.

Your color almost looks pink and white except for the bruises and a little vernix on your face and hair. Because everything is so perfect it is painfully difficult to understand what went wrong. Such a big boy you are—five pounds and eight ounces. We supposed you would only be three or four pounds, coming so soon. And the size of your hands and feet! You don't feel so little as I hold you close.

You are just the right size. There is pain and pleasure in knowing your body, the knees and feet that kicked. We can hold you once, bathe you, dress you. And then we'll say goodbye, keeping only the memory of you and some mementos.

Your body will soon be gone, but the love goes on forever.

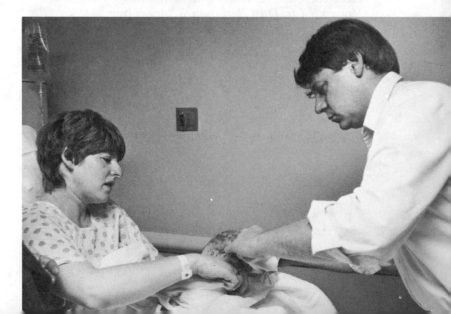

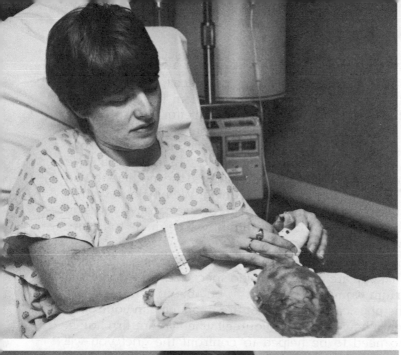

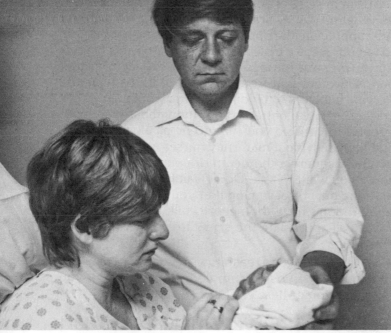

And we loved you
all of your life.

Love,

Mom

WHERE SHOULD YOU RECEIVE YOUR CARE?

In the past mothers of stillborns or critically ill babies were automatically placed on a ward away from the postpartum area of the hospital. This was done in an effort to protect the grieving mother from the harsh reality that her baby died while other babies lived. That practice was consistent with our general approach to neonatal death . . . that of denial. We pretended by our actions, and encouraged the mothers to also believe, that they had not lost anything. We now believe that the most helpful and compassionate care we can give you is on the post partum floor. Every attempt will be made to assure you a private room.

During your brief hospital stay you need to be cared for as the mother you are, by nurses who specialize in caring for the post partum woman. You need to be able to ask questions about the physical changes that are happening in your body and to learn how to care for yourself when you return home. You also need to be helped to confront the grief you will experience from the loss of your baby. Though this approach may seem cruel to you at first, and if given the choice you would gladly appreciate the opportunity to deny what has just happened to your life, we believe that it's a better use of your hospital stay to prepare you for what you can expect from grief rather than to protect you from the pain of it. To hear the sound of crying babies is often difficult for a woman after her child has died. But it is far better to have the sympathetic ear of a nurse around to console you than to be all alone at home when it first happens. Most maternity nurses are now trained to help you face squarely the death of your baby. Let your nurse know if you want to talk. Don't wait for her to bring up the subject. She may be assuming that you have shared with other staff and don't have the need to talk anymore at this moment. She will appreciate the signal from you and will be ready to respond.

If, after hearing all the good reasons we have for keeping you under our wing on the postpartum floor, you still think you would rest better somewhere else, please let us know.

THE BEST CARE WE CAN GIVE YOU
IS NOT
TO PROTECT YOU FROM PAIN
BUT
TO SUPPORT YOU THROUGH IT

WHEN CAN YOU START HAVING INTERCOURSE AGAIN?

One way for couples to comfort each other in their sorrow is by making love. It seems unfair for you to have to deny yourself one of the few things that can give you some joy at such a sad time in your life. Most doctors agree that you should wait at least two weeks before you resume intercourse after the birth of a child. This delay does not need to prevent you from loving and being close in other ways that do not involve intercourse. You need each other right now so don't neglect to show love through kissing, carressing and holding.

When you do resume intercourse, remember to protect yourself from becoming pregnant again too soon by using a form of birth control acceptable to you.

Communication between the two of you is essential at this time. While one of you may want to make love for comfort, the other may dread it for fear of similar complications in a future pregnancy, or from guilt for having pleasure at such a sad time, or because of memories of how the dead child was created.

THE POST-PARTUM VISIT(S)

There are five reasons for going back to the physician for a follow-up visit after you have been discharged from the hospital.

The first is to check that your physical progress has been normal, that the uterus is returning to normal size, that the surgical wounds (episiotomy or cesarean section) are healing normally, that your breasts are not engorged or infected and that the bodily functions have returned to normal.

The second reason is to review the pregnancy. You will want to go over the details of your prenatal and hospital care to try and understand the reasons why your baby died. The autopsy report will be available for review and may give you more information.

In very general terms, there are three main causes of infant death close to the time of delivery. The most common cause of death is immaturity. Sometimes this is preventable, sometimes not. The second most common cause of death is congenital abnormality. Again, sometimes the cause is apparent but very often there is no obvious reason why a certain abnormality developed. The third cause is the general category related to maternal illness such as pre-eclampsia, hypertension or diabetes. In spite of increasing understanding of the causes of unexpected death, there still remains situations where no clear explanation can be given.

Whatever the cause, there are probably two main questions you will want answered. These are, "could we have done anything differently" and, "is it likely to happen again."

This second question points to a third reason for coming to a follow-up visit. Sometimes in the future you may want to plan another pregnancy. When the time comes you will want to be properly prepared for it and that preparation begins with as complete an understanding as possible of why your baby died in this recent pregnancy. For instance, it may be that an x-ray of the uterus will be necessary to see if there is a problem in the uterus that causes premature labor or perhaps you should discuss the possibility of an amniocentesis being performed in the next pregnancy.

The fourth reason for coming is to help you to select the most suitable method of contraception if you wish to use one.

The fifth reason for a check-up is that your physician will want to know that you have started the normal grief process. If the process has been delayed or distorted, or you are not receiving emotional support from your family and friends, this is the time to recognize it so that appropriate intervention can be recommended.

There is quite a lot to accomplish in your follow-up visit. Don't be surprised if it isn't all dealt with in one visit. Usually it is better not to try to conceive again immediately so the details of planning for another pregnancy may be better left until a time further removed from your baby's death.

The time for your visits will be decided by your physician according to individual circumstances. Often times the doctor will try to arrange your appointment around the time the baby's final autopsy report is completed so the findings can be explained to you while you are in the office. This would be at approximately one month after leaving the hospital. Often, an earlier appointment is appropriate.

MICHAEL

There is a child somewhere
Lost in earth
Or time,
He was mine.

There is no other feeling
Like the movement of an unborn child.
It's closer
Than someone touching you
From the outside.
It's purely and cleanly
And clearly
Your own moment.

For those few months
We were together,
Alone against the world.
But nature,
That grand cheat,
Took him away
When we needed each other most.

I cannot say why I could not save him.
Could there be a reason why?
Did my body reject him in its humiliation?
Did I, in my mind, push him away?
Because he wouldn't let me give up
When I wanted to?
I carried him
And He carried me
Through a time when we could not go alone.

It doesn't matter now to anyone.
No one ever knew.
But now and then,
Along the day,
I look at first graders
With their Snoopy lunchboxes
And tender paintings of trees and frogs,
And I think about those first feelings
Of movement
And growth.

Merrit Malloy

FORGIVE ME, MY SON

Forgive me if I do not cry
The day you die
The simplest reason that I know is
Fathers are not supposed to cry
I figured you would expect me
To be strong
To act the way I would have
Taught you
Forgive me, my son, if I do not cry
The day you die . . .
Forgive me
If I do . . .

MARIAH DEAR

Until you I never knew there
   were so many babies.
I see them everywhere . . . babies in arms,
   at grocery stores, church, the park, on our block.
I am guessing but somehow know
   some are just your days had you stayed.
Mothers stare sometimes because I do . . .
   one looked curious so I asked,
"How old?" And she was one month
   later than you born.
I shall always see you . . . little girls
   at ten . . . later the blush and
   bloom of teens . . . then the coming
   of grace and dignity of woman.
But wait, lest I forget in fleeting time
   how soon I shall know you.

By Kate McNassar
Mariah's grandmother

"A FATHER IS MUCH MORE THAN A PARENT. HE IS ONE WHO WILL HELP YOU IN MANY WAYS. IN MOST CASES HE WILL SUCCEED."
– ALBERT

A NOTE TO FATHERS

Like Albert (above), most fathers themselves are accustomed to the idea that they can supply whatever help is needed in almost any situation. But after the death of your baby, you as a father are likely to experience similar feelings of helplessness, guilt, anger and lack of motivation that your wife feels.

For too long the father has been left out of the picture in the birth or death of the baby. Only in very recent times has it been recognized that you too, have been forming an attachment to your baby. You will also need to grieve so that you can loosen the attachment in time.

One of the sad times for you will be when people ask how your wife is doing because they realize how great a loss it is to her, but they forget that you're hurting too. They forget that the baby is as much yours as hers, that even though it is in her body that the baby grows, it took both of you to start this new life on its way. Your emotions and indeed your very life were also changing as our made room in your life for the expected new person.

Find a friend with whom you can talk comfortably. Self-help groups are an excellent way for fathers to find other fathers who are dealing with common problems.

While your wife is in the hospital, the hospital staff and others may look to you to make certain decisions: Do either of you want to see or hold the baby? How will the funeral arrangements be handled and by whom? Resist the impulse to make swift decisions by yourself. Don't assume that you will be easing her burdens by protecting her from having to share these decisions. These choices are best handled together and it is important to take your time to decide.

One of the strange things about grief is that it is too intensely personal to be completely shared. You are in it together…but alone. Though you support and comfort each other you cannot lessen the intensity of each other's pain. This can be worrying and frustrating and sometimes introduce surprising strains and stresses into your marital relationship.

GRANDPARENTS GRIEVE TOO

Your own parents are hurting too. They grieve for the grandchild they will never get to play with and to watch grow. And they grieve for you, their child. There is probably nothing they would rather do for you right now than take away your suffering. That's how it is with parents. Just as you didn't want your little baby to suffer, your own parents will want to protect you from the cruelty of grief. Most parents never get over the desire to protect their children.

It will be hard for them to watch you take the death of your baby so hard. They may say or do things to try to make you feel better. Be patient with them if they don't understand what you are feeling and therefore do the "wrong thing."

THE FUNCTION OF FRIENDS IS TO BE THE SOUNDING BOARD FOR GRIEF.

HOME AND FRIENDS

What about after you get home? The hospital environment may have contributed to a sense of unreality regarding your loss. But the reality of the situation will hit you hard when you are back in the familiar surroundings of home. The sense of loss will be more real, the pain more acute, the reminders that the baby is "missing" more obvious. Even so, you may still feel somewhat distant or remote from things, and you may find it difficult to settle back into your usual routine. Don't let yourself worry about this. The adjustment will take time, and it is neither wise nor helpful to deliberately busy yourself with tasks that you are not interested in just so you can "forget about the baby," which of course you cannot do anyway.

You may have already arranged a nursery or a special place for the baby, a place filled with toys and little garments for the baby. Even if others offer to take care of putting away all those painful reminders before you get home, ask them not to. This is a task which you should save for yourself—for when you are ready. There is no "right" time for tending to this. You will know when it is time.

Your family and friends will most likely react in different ways. Ideally a time of grief such as this is when the love and support of the family circle really comes through, and you will receive the benefit of that support. However, don't be surprised by some responses from your family. Even those closest to you may feel embarrassed or uncomfortable talking about the baby and will wait for signals from you that "it's okay." Sometimes others will become impatient when you don't "get over it" quickly. Or they will suggest that you forget about the tragedy and start planning for your next child. All of these attitudes, and others, can be hurtful to you because they imply a lack of understanding of your feelings for this baby and a lack of acceptance of your baby as a real person. But try to understand how it happens that others respond in these ways and "forgive them for they know not what they do." They had not formed the bond or attachment to your baby that you had, and it is inevitable that their grief will be less intense, and that therefore some of their actions and words will seem thoughtless and cruel.

You may find yourself dreading having your best friend speak glowingly about her pregnancy. On the other hand, she may be reluctant to talk to you at all about her pregnancy for fear of hurting you. You will have to decide for yourself what is the best way for you to handle this. Again, there is nothing wrong with simply telling your friend what you need.

Remember, you must educate people about how you feel and what you need from them. If it hasn't happened to them, they probably just don't know what to do. You may want to share this booklet with them.

Society has some built-in hurts in store for you. Phone calls offering free diaper service or special introductory offers on baby products will be annoying. The mail will bring parenting magazines, insurance proposals, photo offers, etc. By writing to Direct Mail Marketing in New York City you may be able to cut down on most of the unwanted reminders of your baby's death.

Obtain the address from your local post office to have your name removed from these mailing lists.

WHAT CAN YOU EXPECT FROM CHILDREN

As in every experience in life, childrens' reactions to death and grief will be unpredictable. Their ages, previous experiences with death, and their expectations for a brother or sister will play a role in their responses.

31

Be prepared for the honesty and directness which young children will bring to conversations about their baby's death. Facts are important building blocks for their future understanding. Clear and direct answers to their questions are the best. Give them only the information they ask for. And don't be surprised if they bring up the subject again and again.

Young children don't see death as permanent. Expect to hear statements like "Is the baby still dead?", or "Can I play with the baby tomorrow?" Young children are more affected by a disruption in their environment and daily routines than they are about the death of a sibling they haven't yet met. Many children will be concerned that the mother might also die, possibly that they themselves might die if they get sick. Visits to mom in the hospital or occasional phone calls will be reassuring.

Though it is indeed a blessing to have other children at home, it is possible that your responsibility for their care will tend to frustrate you as you move through the natural grieving process. If you are crying or acting angry or upset, explain as best you can the reason why. Make sure your children understand that you are upset because the baby died and not because of anything they may have done. Children are far more capable of understanding such things than we generally give them credit.

Take your cues from your children. Do they want to see their dead sibling or will a picture satisfy their curiosity? Do they want to be present at the funeral service? Given the choices, children don't usually put themselves in situations they aren't ready to handle. Denying them the right to make these choices may set up greater fears of death in the future.

BUT YOU ARE THERE, AN INVISIBLE ASPECT OF YOU REMAINS WITH ME.

ANNIVERSARIES, HOLIDAYS AND BIRTHDAYS CAN BE ESPECIALLY DIFFICULT

One of the sad realities is that you will remember while others will forget. Anniversaries of your baby's birth and death days may go unnoticed and unobserved even by your friends and family, while you anticipate them with pain and dread.

And it probably won't even occur to them that you may be sensitive and hesitant about participating in family reunions following the death of your baby, or that such occasions can magnify your feelings of sadness. You can help in such situations by reminding your friends and family ahead of time so that they can prepare to be supportive to you when you need them to be. Don't "set them up" to fail and don't "set yourself up" for disappointment by saying nothing.

Some parents make a point of doing something special on the anniversary of their child's death, as a way of remembering the child. Why not contribute altar flowers to your church during the anniversary week, or send a contribution to your favorite charity in your child's name, or even make a birthday cake and celebrate?

Some parents anticipate the sense of depression that can come especially at Christmas, and make special ornaments for their Christmas tree that remind them and others about their lost child. In this way the absent child is "included" with the rest of the children in the festivities associated with the holiday.

THERE ARE NO BEST WAYS.
THERE ARE ONLY ALTERNATIVES

WAYS TO CELEBRATE THE BIRTH AND DEATH OF YOUR BABY

Formal recognition of a person's life is important to those who were close to that person. That is why we have funerals, wakes, memorial tributes, etc. Such recognition is no less important for a baby who lived only a few minutes or hours. In the past, hospital personnel were wrong in thinking that the "best thing" for parents was to remove the memories of their tragedy as quickly as possible. We used to think that parents couldn't afford the emotional or financial cost of saying goodbye. So we did it for them.

Now we know, from talking to many parents, that parents never forget. It makes a lot more sense for you the parents to take the time and find the ways to say goodbye. You will find the results personally satisfying and helpful to you in the total grief process.

As you read further you will learn about many different ways to say goodbye. Some will cost a lot. Some will cost only a little. We ask you to consider which of these seems right for you and for your baby. You may also use these suggestions as a take-off point for some special ideas of your own.

DECISIONS NEED TO BE MADE

Shortly after your baby's birth and death you will be confronted with some decisions about what is to be done with your child's body. Though some decisions can wait, you probably should not delay decisions about autopsy and removal to a mortuary for more than one or two days after death. In hospitals where there is no morgue the latter decision will need to be made sooner.

DO YOU WANT AN AUTOPSY PERFORMED?

It is possible that your doctor will request that an autopsy be performed on your baby's body. An autopsy is a careful examination of the internal tissues and organs of the body with the hope of better understanding the cause of death. Frequently stillborns look perfectly healthy and beautiful upon initial routine examination and their appearance offers no clue to the cause of death. We hope the internal examination will provide the desired information. However, in some cases it may not. The procedure may clear up uncertainties in your own mind and provide helpful information for you in planning future pregnancies. Autopsy results may also help the medical community to prevent similar deaths in other newborns.

An autopsy is usually done at the hospital by a pathologist, though some hospitals do not have pathology departments and will need to send the baby somewhere else to have this work done. If you are like most parents you will feel better if you know where the baby is being kept or where the baby is being taken for autopsy, so don't be afraid to ask. If you have made the choice of a mortuary, the pathology department should be notified that someone from the mortuary will come to take the baby's body to the mortuary after the autopsy.

As the child's parents you have the final say as to whether an autopsy will be performed and you must sign a form granting your permission before the work can begin. Also, if you want to limit the autopsy in any way you may do so. For example, some parents ask that no incisions be made on the baby's head. Include such requests in writing on the Autopsy Permit before you sign it.

Even if hospital personnel do not suggest that an autopsy be performed, you have the right to request that it be done.

The cost for an infant autopsy is approximately $75 to $100 though many hospitals will not charge this cost to the family. You may receive a small statement—usually amounting to less than $20—from one of the hospital labs, for procedures

34

connected with the autopsy. Hospitals vary in their billing procedures.

The preliminary results of the autopsy will be available within a day or two. The final report may take a few weeks to complete. Your doctor will go over the results with you and answer any questions you may have at that time. We know you will probably think of other questions to ask later, and we will make ourselves available when you need to talk.

HOW TO FIND A FUNERAL HOME

Your family may have a funeral home that has served your family before, or the hospital may be able to recommend one close by that will help you make arrangements for your baby at a reasonable cost, or you may choose to find one by looking in the yellow pages of the telephone directory. If you plan to bury the baby in a cemetery you might want to find one close to your home, especially if you anitcipate wanting to visit the baby's grave often. Some families have already purchased family plots for all family members to use.

You will find the cost for infant burial much less expensive than for adults. Funeral Home staff appreciate the need for you to make final preparations for your baby while realizing that the financial burden to young families could be overwhelming. Our experience with Funeral Homes has been contrary to the negative image they previously held. We have found them to be most helpful in all aspects of assisting parents.

OPTIONS INVOLVING
FUNERAL ARRANGEMENTS

If you live far from the hospital where your baby died and you plan to have the baby buried in your own town, you may want to take the baby in your own car rather than having the mortuary transport the baby. This can save you money. You need to let the hospital and mortuary know of your plans. You will also want to provide a closed container in which to place the baby. Any sturdy box will do, or you can purchase one from a local mortuary.

If you are going to be transporting the baby across the state line you will need a copy of the baby's death certificate and a permit. A local funeral home can help you obtain this.

If you want to hold your baby after an autopsy has been performed or have an open casket at the funeral service you may want to have the baby embalmed. The purpose of embalming is to prepare the body for viewing and for sanitary reasons. It is not mandatory.

FINANCIAL CONSIDERATIONS

Most parents don't have insurance policies that would cover cost of mortuary services for a baby who has died at birth. However, below is a list of possible resources for you to check out.

COMPANY LIFE INSURANCE through your employer may include your dependents' funeral costs, or a portion of them.

UNIONS may also have some benefits to help you. If you are a veteran your baby may be buried in a National Cemetery at no cost to you, and a grave marker will be provided.

For income tax purposes, if your baby weighed no less than 500 grams and was given a birth certificate, you can claim the baby as a dependent for that year. A stillbirth cannot be claimed.

Costs for funeral arrangements can range from $50.00 to $500.00 and even more depending on your choices. Cemetery plots can greatly increase the overall cost. All these prices are approximate and vary depending on the locale.

Cremation is by far the most economical way to go. You do not need to buy a plot or niche for the cremains unless you want to. You may take your baby's ashes home with you or leave them at the mortuary until you've decided what you want to do with them. Cremation for an infant costs approximately $25.00. Service charges may increase the total cost to $75.00. Some mortuaries generously waive most of the costs for infant cremation.

The ashes will be put in a small cardboard box, unless you provide a container or purchase one from the mortuary. Prices for the containers start around $25.00.

Burial, of course will be more expensive because a casket and plot will have to be purchased and there are costs involved in preparing the gravesite. A casket for an infant will cost between $50.00 and $300.00. Some parents prefer to build the casket themselves. Service fees which include embalming, preparing the gravesite and newspaper notification may cost $100.00 to $300.00.

Occasionally parents want to bury their baby on their own property. In many state this is possible. Contact your local health department or funeral director for more information if you are interested in this option.

You will need to make decisions about what is best for you. Don't let others make the decisions for you.

Contrary to popular belief, there is no set period of time during which all funeral and burial arrangements must be completed. Some hospitals, however, depending on their policies, may want you to choose a mortuary before you leave the hospital. If you are going to remain in the hospital for a few days for your own reasons of health, ask that major decisions be delayed until you are ready to be involved.

IF I HAD A DAY
THAT I COULD GIVE YOU,
I'D GIVE TO YOU A DAY
JUST LIKE TODAY.

WHAT TYPE OF CEREMONY DO YOU WANT TO HELP SAY GOODBYE TO YOUR BABY?

Some parents may want to have a service in the hospital chapel, at the mortuary or at the gravesite. Others will prefer a service in their usual place of worship. If you have no religious affiliation you may prefer to plan an event on your own at a place which has special meaning to you, and with friends who are special to you.

Generally the costs incurred for a formal funeral ceremony include a fee for the services of a clergyperson and additional minimal charges if the funeral is held at the mortuary.

Parents may choose to have the baby's body brought to their home after embalming, either for a funeral service, or for a vigil or for a "wake" prior to funeral service. The term wake describes an old Irish tradition in which friends stay awake to view and be with the one who has died, until the hour of the funeral. Funeral Homes were developed to provide for services and rituals which were originally taken care of in private homes, and many of our great grandparents were "viewed" in the parlor before commercial Funeral Homes were in vogue.

Here is an additional list of requests which parents have told us they wish they had made, before they found it was too late:
* to hold the baby one more time.
* to dress the baby in a special outfit, or wrap the baby in a special blanket.
* to have a special toy placed in the casket with the baby.
* to save a lock of the baby's hair.
* to arrange for a picture to be taken of the child after embalming and before burial.

- to personally handle the tasks of dressing and grooming the child for burial.
- to have a special quilt draped over the casket.
- to have a special reading shared at the funeral service.

WE MUST NOT WALLOW IN OUR MEMORIES OR SURRENDER TO THEM, JUST AS WE DON'T GAZE ALL THE TIME AT A VALUABLE PRESENT. BUT GET IT OUT FROM TIME TO TIME, AND FOR THE REST HIDE IT AWAY AS A TREASURE WE KNOW IS THERE ALL THE TIME. TREATED THIS WAY, THE PAST CAN GIVE US LASTING JOY AND INSPIRATION.

WHERE TO FIND HELP

Getting your life back in order after your baby has died is no easy chore. You may be overwhelmed with the physical and emotional reactions your body will go through. You lack the motivation it takes to work through you grief. You don't know where to start, or what to do to help yourself. You may not know anyone who has gone through a similar experience, and if you do you may be afraid to talk to that person for fear of opening old wounds and causing more pain.

But you needn't be alone through this difficult time in your life. There are professional people available to help you sort out your feelings. There are excellent books on the subject of death. And there are other ordinary people like yourself who are willing to listen because they too have "been there."

HOW DO YOU KNOW IF YOU MAY NEED EXTRA HELP IN WORKING THROUGH YOUR GRIEF?

You may want to consider seeking professional help, especially if you manifest any of the following symptoms.
- you have furious hostility toward someone
- you refuse to be comforted by anyone

- you are having ruminating thoughts of self-destruction
- you are becoming distant from your partner or family and friends
- you are using alcohol or drugs to ease the pain of grief
- you are still having difficulty sleeping or eating even though it's been several weeks since your baby died
- you are unable to speak of your dead baby without experiencing fresh grief even though it's been several weeks since your baby died

Below are some ideas of professional people to whom you may look for help.

PROFESSIONAL WHO CAN HELP:

Your OBSTETRICIAN OR THE FAMILY DOCTOR who was with you when the baby was born may be very helpful to you. You will most likely want to discuss some questions you may have about what happened during your labor and delivery. Don't be reluctant because you think he or she is too busy to talk with you. The death of your baby was very hard on your doctor too and he or she probably needs the opportunity to talk further with you about it.

A SOCIAL WORKER, PSYCHOLOGIST, and or FAMILY COUNSELOR may be helpful to you if you feel the need for some additional counseling. These professionals may be located by looking in the yellow pages under Marriage and Family Counselors, or by calling one of the major hospitals in you area. The hospital's pastoral care or social service department may have information about groups in your area that can help you. Such groups may have lists of professionals whom their members recommend. Keep in mind that not all grief therapists are specifically knowledgeable about perinatal bereavement so you may need to spend some time finding the right match for you.

Don't forget CLERGY. Whether or not you have been affiliated with an organized religious group in the past, you may find yourself now searching for some answers to many of life's puzzles. Seek help through your own pastor or ask the chaplain in your hospital for the name of a minister who can help you.

SELF-HELP GROUPS are now available in most communities. These groups are just what their names suggest - people with similar issues helping each other to come to terms with their plight. Because much of the stress of grief can be relieved by talking about your loss this resource can be a lifesaver. Most of the groups are open ended and you are welcome to attend at any time. The groups are generally facilitated by a bereaved parent who is further along in his or her grief. Many of the groups publish monthly newsletters. Some have "phone buddies", or people who are willing to talk on the phone between meetings. Your hospital social service or local United Way agency should have listing of what's available in your area.

Most parents come to recognize that there is nothing that helps more than being able to talk with someone else who has experienced the death of their child. The loneliness factor of grief is divided when shared. If you are having difficulty locating a group in your area contact the National Share office at (314) 947-6164 or write to:

Pregnancy and Infant Loss Support Inc.,
St. Joseph Health Center,
300 First Capitol Drive, St. Charles, MO 63301.

They keep an updated list of support groups nationwide. They also have available guidelines to starting a local group.

AND THEN THERE ARE BOOKS

Reading is a big help for many bereaved parents. It validates your loss, helps you see you're not alone, and can provide important insights into what you are feeling. Some material may also be able to shed some light on the reason for your baby's death. Lots of parents admit that at first they are unable to concentrate enough to read a full book, while others will devour whatever they can get their hands on.

Your local bookstore most likely carries some books on the grief process in general. There are also some books that are available that are specific to perinatal bereavement but they tend to have a fairly short shelf life. Some parents have found what they needed in used book stores. And many of the support groups have created lending libraries to counter the frustration of not being able to find the right book.

Children are helped by books too. There are books that focus in a general way on what "dead" means. These books help build a good foundation for your child. There are also some that can help the child identify with their own feelings or with yours as you grieve over the loss of your baby. Excellent new books are coming out every year. Reading them together will help your child feel included in the experience of the loss of your baby.

The following are mail order services that have a good selection of books on perinatal bereavement.
Perinatal Loss
2116 N.E. 18th Ave.
Portland, Oregon 97212
(503) 284-7426

Centering Corporation
1531 N. Saddle Creek Rd.
Omaha, NE 68104
(402) 553-1200

Pregnancy and Infant Loss Center
1421 East Wayzata Blvd.
Wayzata, MN 55391
(612) 473-9372

Birth and Life Bookstore
P.O. Box 70625
Seattle, WA 98107
(206) 789-4444

WHEN SHOULD I GET PREGNANT AGAIN?

On this big question regarding your future, advice comes easy. Some well-intentioned observers will suggest that you try again right away, while others will advise that you wait a while. For you, the thought of another pregnancy may bring only expectations of more pain and sorrow. On the other hand the desire to have a child may outweigh those fears.

What we've heard from many bereaved couples in the past is that the decision to try again was easy in comparison to actually living through the nine months that followed. Most parents who did become pregnant shortly after their baby died admitted later that they wished they had waited, though they also acknowledge that no one could have convinced them to do so at the time.

The physical recovery time after an uncomplicated delivery is relatively short. Two months is generally adequate. Emotional recovery after a baby has died is not so easy. We wish we could offer you a simple formula, and guarantee that, if you follow it step by step, in six months time you will be ready to enter into another pregnancy that will be a breeze. But there is no magical time, no proven recipe, and no amnesia to make the next pregnancy easy. Your next pregnancy is bound to be filled with fears and anxieties over its outcome. This is normal. If you are like most parents the next pregnancy will be difficult, but it will not be quite so difficult if you allow yourselves time to rebuild your emotional strength before getting pregnant again so you will be better able to cope with the difficult times.

Because this book is designed only to help you deal with the death of your child it does not include information which would assist you during another pregnancy. We have therefore prepared a second book, **Still To Be Born—A Guide For Bereaved Parents During A Subsequent Pregnancy** to help you anitcipate that experience.

YOU MUST HELP TIME DO ITS HEALING

Time alone will not heal your broken heart. You, yourself, and only you are the one to decide if you will allow time to heal your wounds. Some people never get over the death of their child, while others are working at remembering yesterday and creating tomorrow. Here are some things to remember and do as you "work" with time.

1. **Take time to grieve.** Don't bury yourself with activity just so you can avoid having to think about your baby. Instead, set aside some time to be alone to deal with your feelings, however painful they may be.

2. **Put off major decisions for at least a year.** Delay changing jobs or moving to another town until you feel certain that you have really come to terms with your grief.

3. **Talk to others.** Let your friends know how you feel. Tell them what you need. Seek out others who have also had an experience similar to your own.

4. **Be patient with your partner.** Remember, everyone experiences grief in his own way. He may not be showing grief in the same way you do, but that does not mean he is not also feeling the loss deeply.

5. **Don't plan to get pregnant right away.** You can't suc- cessfully say hello to your next baby until you have said goodbye to this baby . . . and saying goodbye takes time. You

42

can't "replace" one baby with another. Even through the desire to be a parent is very strong, give yourself time.

6. **Allow your next child to be his own person.** Choose a new name. Don't imply that the new child is a replacement for this dead child by "saving" the old name. It rightly belongs to your dead child. Each child deserves to have a special place in hour heart.

7. **Be patient with yourself.** Don't be disturbed if you aren't getting over "it" as quickly as you had hoped. Assume that what you are experiencing is normal. Bizarre delusions can be expected. Let yourself be inconsistent. Relapses are normal too.

8. **Do something with your feelings.** Write about how you are feeling. Sew something you had planned to make for the baby. Build or make a special box to place memories of your baby in. Design the headstone for your baby's grave. Make a stitchery of your baby's name, birthdate, weight and length.

9. **Design and send announcements of your baby's short life** to your friends and family. This might be a good way for you to recognize your baby's life no matter how short.

10. **Exercise.** Even if you don't feel like it. Exercise won't relieve your grief, but it will release some of the pent up stress of grief.

11. **Reach out to others who are in need.** You may think you have nothing to offer until you've tried.

NOT EVERYTHING THAT IS FACED CAN BE CHANGED, BUT NOTHING CAN BE CHANGED UNTIL IT IS FACED.

George Baldwin

THE BROWN STAR STORY

Not long ago, astronomers found in the heavens gaseous celestial bodies – clouds of cosmic dust – which they think have finally answered the mystery of what exists between the small things in the universe, like planets, and the bigger things, like the sun. They call this cosmic dust "brown dwarfs" or "pre-stars", because although brown dwarfs have all the elements to become a star, for some reason they never did.

All stars go on to live full lives, from their hot, bright white dwarf stage to their aged cooler and dimmer red giant stage. But "brown stars" only go so far. Instead of being born to live a normal star's life, they remain cool and dim, hiding in the heavens, sprinkled in clusters among the other stars 150 light years from Earth.

But like our babies, their roles in the universe are very important. In fact, scientists believe they serve as a link between the small things and the big things, holding the universe together: a mid-point between the beginning and ending of our universal story.

As we grieve for our babies who died before reaching stardom of their earthly lives, perhaps we can find comfort in the possibility that they were designated for this very special universal role. Energized by our love, they are guardians of our memories of what was and our dreams of what some day may be.

As we look to the heavens, seeking answers, we send messages of love to our "brown star" babies.

Kim Steffgen

44

THE SITTING TIME

Don't listen to the foolish unbelievers
  who say forget.
Take up your armful of roses and
  remember them
  the flower and the fragrance.
When you go home to do your sitting
  in the corner by the clock
  and sip your rosethorn tea
It will warm your face and fingers
  and burn the bottom of your belly.
But as her gone-ness piles in white,
  crystal drifts,
It will be the blossom of her moment
  the warmth on your belly,
  the tiny fingers unfolding,
  the new face you've always known,
That has changed you.
Take her moment, and hold it
  As every mother does.
    She will always be
    your daughter
And when the sitting is done you'll find
  bitter grief could never poison
  the sweetness of her time.

Joe Digman

WHAT WE REMEMBER LIVES ON.

45

ONE MONTH LATER

"Where is your baby?"   Until yesterday the joyful, expectant look which accompanied the question, started me to crying. It's only today, one month later, that I can reply, with peace in my heart, that our baby is gone, that he died before he was born.

*Physically I am healed. My body has forgotten the pregnancy, but my mind is still letting go. The empty, sad feelings have lessened and there are more times when it is possible to laugh or just to feel at peace. Getting to sleep at night is easier now than it was that first week. But fixing meals and eating them is still a chore. I've learned that eating sugar, or consuming alcoholic beverages or skipping meals can bring my mood crashing to the floor. The anger which I didn't feel so much at first now comes out suddenly in the form of irritability with David and the kids, especially when I am tired. Fortunately I have taken time off from work to just take care of myself. Writing down how I feel in my journal and exercising regularly both help me to get through the day without being overwhelmed by my feelings of depression and anger. I talk for hours with friends, totally unaware of the time passing. Right now there is only one reality, loss and grief. The greeting card companies and people in general expect that each day will get a little easier and a little brighter for people in my situation. But that's not exactly how grief works. For me the days are unpredictable. Some days it seems like every woman I see is pregnant or carrying a newborn baby. **It's just so unfair.** On other days I remember vividly what Tony looked like, and I feel again the love and peace we shared at his birth.*

Loving Tony has brought David and me closer. I am so grateful we can share this burden. I am told that time will heal the grief but now I know that it is taking the time to grieve that heals.

Kathryn Castricano

46

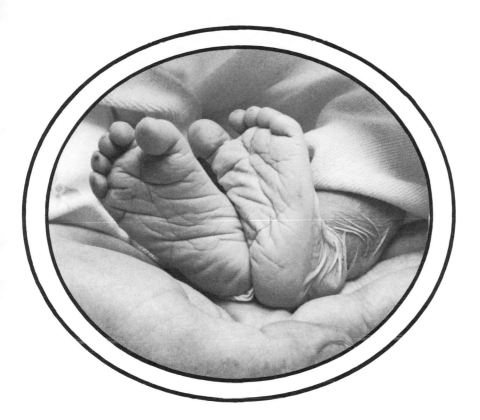

OUR JOYS WILL BE GREATER
OUR LOVE WILL BE DEEPER
OUR LIFE WILL BE FULLER
BECAUSE WE SHARED YOUR MOMENT

When words don't come easy......

The birthday of your child is important, even if your child died too soon. You still may want to send a birth announcment that let's people know of your child's brief life. These 3.5"x 5" cards are a special way to help your friends and relatives know about and share your sorrow. We offer you a choice of two different types of cards:

Standard birth announcements
The inside of the card is similar to that of any typical birth announcement, except that an additional space is provided for you to fill in your child's death date. On the front of the card we print your choice of a,b,c,d, or e below. ($7.00 for a pkg of 10.)

Personalized birth announcements
You give us all the information that you want included in your message and we do the rest. Your return address is printed on the envelopes at no extra charge. (Minimum order 2 packages @ $14.00/pkg.)

FRONT OF CARD: *available only for personalized cards*

Choose one of these sayings or write one of your own:

  a. *"A person's a person no matter how small."*

  b. *"Hold close these moments for we shall always live by remembering."*

  c. *"Unto us a child is born, a special child for a special reason. We don't pretend to understand, only to accept and to love."*

  d. *"But love goes on forever."*

  e. *"Our joys will be greater, our love will be deeper, our lives will be fuller, because we shared (his her,their) moment(s).*

  *f. *"She (he) is precious in the eyes of God."*

  *g. *"And in a twinkling of an eye this little one came into our hearts."*

  *h. *"Our dreams are sure gonna miss him (her)."*

  *i. *"Some people only dream of angels. We held one in our hands."*

  *j. *"What we remember lives on."*

  *k. *Your own message*

INSIDE OF PERSONALIZED CARD:

The following are sample verses. You may choose one, combine phrases, or create your own. Call us if you have questions or need other suggestions.

l.   Our baby, (name) was born on (date) and died on (date). Even though she was with us for only a short time, we loved her very much. (parent's names)

m.   (Parent's names) sadly announce the birth and death of their son, (name) on (date and time) wt. 5lb 12 oz length 19 1/2 in. We will love him always.

n.   Our baby, (name) was stillborn on (date and time). He will be sadly missed by his brother, (name) his sisters, (names) and his parents, (names)

o.   We are sad to announce the short life of our daughter, (name). She came and went in an instant on (date) taking with her a lifetime of hopes and dreams we had for her. We will hold her in our hearts forever. (parent's names)

p.   Our baby girls, (names) were stillborn on (date). We will miss the warmth of their touch, the chorus of their voices, and the patter of their feet. But their love will live forever. (parents)

q.   Because we know you care about us, we want you to know that on (date) our wished for baby passed quickly through our lives. We are saddened, but remain hopeful that someday soon our dream of having a child will be fulfilled. (parents names)

r.   Our twins, (names) were born (date). (Name) died shortly after birth. We are happy to report that her sister is gaining weight and will be coming home soon. (Name) will always be remembered by her (twin sister, parents)

BACK OF CARD

The following message is included on the back of standard announcements, but is optional on personalized announcements:

Dear Friend,
Acknowledgement of our baby's short life may be upsetting to you. You may think the less said the better. Until now we did not know how important it would be for us to tell you of our baby even though our baby died. You can help us through this difficult time by letting us talk about our sorrow when we feel the need, allowing us to cry when we want, and not pretending everything's okay... when it's not. It will take time, but with your support we will make it.

ORDER FORM

We know how important it is for you to get the information about your baby's death to your friends as soon as possible. To order, tear out and mail this order form. We will make every effort to fill your order and return it by priority mail within 24 hours after we receive it. Phone (503 284-7426)or Fax (503 282-8985) orders are also accepted using your VISA or Mastercard.

NAME:_____

ADDRESS:_____

CITY;_____STATE____ZIP:_____

PHONE: (___)_____

STANDARD ANNOUNCEMENTS_____

Quantity desired: _____packs of 10 @ $7.00 per pack,
                  including envelopes   _____

        stillborn_____ neonatal death_____
        boy____ girl____

        Circle choice of message for front of card:

                a   b   c   d   e

PERSONALIZED ANNOUNCEMENTS____

Quantity desired: ____ packs @ $14.00 per pack
                  (minimum: 2 packs) incl. envelopes   _____

        message on back: Yes____ No____
        (enter personal information on the back of this
        form)

                        POSTAGE AND HANDLING_____
                ($3.50 for first 2 packs; add .75 for each additional pack)

                                        TOTAL_____

Mail to: Perinatal Loss, 2116 NE 18th, Portland, OR 97212, or
phone: (503) 284-7426 to place your order.

FRONT OF PERSONALIZED CARD
Circle your choice of sayings:

a   b   c   d   e   f   g   h   i   j   k

OR, print or type your own statement below, exactly as you want it to appear on the front of the folder:

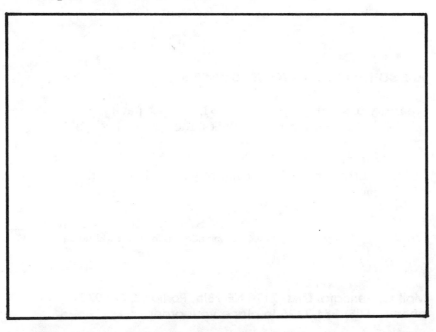

INSIDE OF PERSONALIZED CARD

Using suggestions l through r above, or developing your own, print or type in the space below, the words which you would like to have printed inside the card.